Everett Gill, Jr.

Marshall,

Mo.

1927

School of Divinity

Gardner-Webb University
School of Divinity

This book donated
by

MARS HILL COLLEGE

TOLERANCE

TOLERANCE

Two Lectures

ADDRESSED TO THE STUDENTS OF SEVERAL OF THE
DIVINITY SCHOOLS OF THE PROTESTANT
EPISCOPAL CHURCH

BY

PHILLIPS BROOKS

With an Introduction by

NICHOLAS MURRAY BUTLER

NEW YORK
E. P. DUTTON & COMPANY
681 FIFTH AVENUE

CONTENTS

TOLERANCE

INTRODUCTION

TOLERANCE is an affair of the spirit, while toleration describes a course of conduct. At a time when both tolerance and toleration are sadly to seek it is becoming and highly useful to bring again to public attention this precious little volume by Phillips Brooks. His spiritual insight was so keen and so penetrating, his interpretation so reasonable and so complete, and his eloquence so stirring that in these latter days there should be a nation-wide reading of this book.

It is in highest degree depressing and not a little remarkable that among a people and under a government where freedom of worship, freedom of conscience and freedom of speech are embedded in the rock of fundamental law, there should now exist organizations whose sole aim is persecution, and that there should be many thousands of individuals who, singly and in groups, constantly manifest an un-American and un-Christian spirit in their attitude, their language and their acts toward those who differ from them even as to relatively minor matters. The preaching and the teaching of Christianity are apparently quite futile with all such; the spirit of Christ has wholly departed from them. Any comprehension of the underlying principles of American government and American social order is quite beyond the ken of all such; they are Prussian-minded and Russian-minded persons, in the sense that they act as did the Prussian militarists, and as the Russian communists still do, toward all who venture to dissent from their views and practices. The persecuting tendency is a distinctive mark of a barbarous people. These persons though living in the twentieth century in a free land and in communities where there are both churches and schools are, none the less, barbarians. Dean Inge sagely remarked that ancient civilizations were destroyed by imported barbarians, whereas we breed our own. Dr. Johnson in his Dictionary remarked of tolerance that though a good word it was not used. Perhaps one might now add that while tolerance is still a good word it is not practiced.

That tolerance which leads to genuine

toleration is a mark of a well balanced mind and temper. It does not mean indifference to truth or weakness in seeking and defending truth. What it means is that the tolerant person, realizing the dignity and the worth of the individual human spirit, grants to each and every human being the right which he claims for himself, namely, to shape his own convictions and his own beliefs in his own way. Argument not force, persuasion not punishment, are his instruments of approach to those whom he would bring to his own way of thinking. As George Eliot once pointed out, the responsibility of tolerance lies with those who have the wider vision.

Unhappily the time through which we are passing is one in which by a few wild words it is possible to make tens of thousands of the ignorant intolerant of him who knows, tens of thousands of the unthrifty and the poor intolerant of him who is thrifty and has gained possessions, and tens of thousands of those who have failed through defects of their own mind and their own character intolerant of him who has succeeded by brains and untiring devotion to a well considered purpose.

Men cannot long live together in an orderly society without toleration, and there can be no genuine toleration, other than the toleration which springs from indifference, unless it be the outgrowth of tolerance.

A careful reading of this little book and reflection upon its teachings ought to quiet some of the intolerant clamor and stop some of the intolerant acts that now surround us on every hand. Much of the present day discussion of the fundamental truths of religion, of philosophy and of the social order is quite unscholarly, and is carried on in apparent ignorance of all that has been said and done with reference to these subjects for some twenty-five hundred years. If there were more scholarship in respect of these matters perhaps there would be more silence.

NICHOLAS MURRAY BUTLER

Columbia University
  in the City of New York
    February 22, 1924

FIRST LECTURE.

GENTLEMEN :

I HAVE accepted with grateful pleasure the privilege of meeting you upon two evenings and talking to you upon Tolerance. I chose that subject because I had long vaguely thought of lecturing upon it, and also because it seemed to me as if there were no group of men to whom one could so fitly speak upon it as a gathering of students of theology. To them more than to other men must come the puzzling problems and interesting suggestions which the whole subject of tolerance involves.

I want to speak this evening about the nature and the history and the hope of tolerance. In my other lecture I should

like to see the applications of what I shall
have said to-day to some of the special
conditions of our time and of our Church.
So we can come nearest to covering the
ground.

I call my subject Tolerance, not Toleration.   Tolerance is a disposition: Toleration is the behavior in which that
disposition finds expression.   A disposition is to its appropriate behavior as a
man is to his shadow.   The shadow repre-
sents the man, but it often misrepresents
him.   It is larger than he is, or smaller.   It
runs before him, or it lags behind him,
according as he stands related to the light
which casts it.   We sometimes have to
guess at what the man is by his shadow;
and so we are constantly having to guess
at men's dispositions by their behavior.
But we never can let ourselves forget that
the disposition is the living thing; and so
to it our thought and study must be
given.   Therefore I speak of tolerance,
and not of toleration.

In studying first, then, the nature of tolerance, that much-belauded and much-misrepresented grace of our own time, we want to start with this assertion, — which is, indeed, the key-assertion of all I have to say, — that it is composed of two elements, both of which are necessary to its true existence, and on the harmonious and proportionate blending of which the quality of the tolerance which is the result depends. These elements are, first, positive conviction; and second, sympathy with men whose convictions differ from our own. Does it sound strange to claim that both these elements are necessary to make a true tolerance? Have we been in the habit of thinking that strong, positive conviction was almost incompatible with tolerance? Have we perhaps been almost afraid to yield to the temptation to let ourselves go into the tolerant disposition of our time, because it seemed to us as if there were no place there for that sure and strong belief which we knew was the first necessity of a strong human life? It would not be strange if we had all felt such a fear. It would be strange if any of us had entirely escaped it, so studiously, so constantly, so earnestly has the world been assured that positive faith and tolerance have no fellowship with one another. "The only foundation for tolerance," said Charles James Fox, "is a degree of scepticism." Not many months ago a most respected clergyman of my own town, speaking at the dedication of a statue of John Harvard in the university which bears his name, declared of the Puritans by whom that college was created: "They were intolerant, as all men, the world over, in all time, have always been, and will always be, when they are in solemn earnest for truth or error." I think that those are melancholy words. The historical fact is melancholy enough. That fact we must grant as mainly true, though not without fair and notable exceptions; but to foretell that man will never come to the condi-

tion in which he can be earnest and tolerant
at once, — that is beyond all things melancholy; that spreads a darkness over all
the future, and obliterates man's brightest
hope. That condemns mankind to an endless choice between earnest bigotry and
tolerant indifference, — or, rather, to an
endless swinging back and forth between
the two in hopeless discontent, in everlasting despair of rest. Against all such
statements of despair we want to take the
strongest ground. We want to assert most
positively that so far from earnest personal conviction and generous tolerance
being incompatible with one another, the
two are necessary each to each. "It is
the natural feeling of all of us," said Fred-
erick Maurice in one of those utterances
of his which at first sound like paradoxes,
and by and by seem to be axioms, — " it is
the natural feeling of all of us that charity
is founded upon the *uncertainty* of truth.
I believe it is founded on the *certainty* of
truth."

One token that this is true is that only with both these elements present in it does tolerance become a clear, definable, respectable position for a man to stand in, an honorable quality for a character to possess. Dr. Holmes, in his Life of Mr. Emerson, declares that "the word 'tolerance' is an insult as applied by one set of well-behaved people to another." No doubt there are insulting tones enough in which the word may be used; but the word itself is not insulting. It expresses a perfectly legitimate and honorable relation between two minds and natures which there is no other word to express. Here is my friend with whom I entirely agree; his thoughts and convictions are the same as mine. I do not tolerate him; there is no place for toleration there. Here is my other friend, who disagrees with me entirely. I disagree with him. But I respect him; I want him to be true to his convictions; and while I claim the right and duty of arguing with him and trying to show him that I am

right, and he is wrong, I would not silence
him by violence if I could. I would not
for the world have him say that he thinks
I am right before his reason is convinced.
Now, that is tolerance. Is there any insult
there? Is not that a recognizable, manly
position for me to stand in as regards my
friend? Is either his manhood or mine
injured or despised? But is it not clear
also that the healthiness of this tolerance
which is in me toward him depends on its
integrity? It is because both its elements
are there that it is a sound condition,
worthy of his soul and mine. Take either
away, and the element which is left becomes
insulting. But then it is not tolerance which
is insulting; for this is not tolerance; for
tolerance is the meeting in perfect harmony of earnest conviction and personal
indulgence.

Whoever has thoughtfully observed human life, knows very well that any quality,
which for its fullest perfectness involves
two elements, will almost certainly present

strange and perplexing complications before it comes to its complete condition.
Strange indeed is the method of the
moral progress of mankind. Not as the
ship sails, moving through the water
evenly, all together, every part keeping
pace with every other part; rather as the
man walks, bringing forward first one side
and then the other, one side being at any
given moment in advance of the other,
equilibrium being always lost and regained
again a little farther on, to be re-lost again
immediately: so, as the man walks, does the
moral progress of mankind advance. Thus
it is that conviction of truth and allowance
of dissent are never in perfect balance and
proportion to each other; now one and
now the other of them is always in advance,
as the whole man in this uneven, sidelong
fashion moves unsteadily forward toward
the time when he shall be tolerant of his
fellow-men just in proportion to the earnestness with which he holds his own well-
proven truth.

This leads to certain complications which it will be well to notice, because they very often, as I think, confuse our thought on the whole subject, and seem to leave us all adrift. Here are two men who stand and look out together over the whole world of opinion. They are not a part of it, for neither of them has any real opinions of his own. They are like men who stand together on a seashore rock and look out over the ocean. It is nothing to them which way the waves are running, and how they cross and recross each other in tumultuous confusion. It is nothing to these men how other men are thinking. They are entirely indulgent. They call themselves, and the world calls them, tolerant. And now suppose that one of those men gets a conviction: he becomes thoroughly in earnest for something which he believes is true. What is the immediate result? Almost certainly there comes a chill and a reserve in his indulgence. Now it appears to him to be a dreadful thing

that other men should think so wrongly.
All the indifference is gone, and the man
is almost more than man, almost divinely
true and sound, if he is not betrayed by
his earnestness into some sort of bigotry,
some intolerant wish toward these men
who are in error. He lifts the axe, or
lights the fire of persecution. Meanwhile
there stands his brother where he used to
stand, still smiling his universal smile, and
saying benignly to all the creeds and here-
sies and opinions, " God bless you every
one," because he has no real creed or
opinions, or even a genuine hearty heresy
of his own. And now which of these two
men shall we praise? Beyond all doubt
the man of earnestness, the man of positive
faith. But then he is a bigot! Will you
praise Torquemada, standing in triumph
beside his burning victims in the market-
place in Seville, more than Montaigne, a
century later, sitting in his library at Paris
and patronizing all the faiths of which he
believed not one, all of which in his soul

he despised? If Torquemada ever had
been like Montaigne, and had come to be
a persecutor out of pure conviction, then
horrible as is this which he is doing, awful
as is the lurid flame which lights his virtue,
I must count that he has made true progress; for these two good things are in him,
— first, a firm belief in something as the
truth of God; and next, a passionate desire that the truth of God should reign
upon the earth.

But what then? We know that this is
not final. This praise of the bigot is not
praise of bigotry. We are thankful for
the traveller that he has left the City of
Destruction and that he is on the way to
the New Jerusalem; but none the less we
feel the misery of the Slough of Despond
through which he is struggling on the way.
Our Inquisitor has made a real advance
from the easy tolerance in which he used
to live; but it has been as if, having started
on his journey, he went back to get one
part of his equipment without which his

journey could not successfully be made.
The man who thus goes on shore again to
get his sails, creeps out of the harbor behind the other sailless boat, which is only
drifting on the tide; but nevertheless he
is nearer to the ultimate haven which they
both are seeking, for the boat that has no
sails will never come there at all. So, to
state it quite without a figure, there are
times when the intolerant man, in virtue,
not of his intolerance, but of that which
for the time has caused him to be intolerant, is farther on toward the ultimate
tolerance than his indulgent brother who
stands in horror at his bigotry. Such is
the curious complication which often marks
men's development on the world's progress in any good attainment. There
comes a seeming loss of that which is all
the time being gained. It is like the circles on an eddying stream. There is one
point in the circle which the eddy makes,
one drop of the stream's water, which is
distinctly going backward, going up the

stream. It seems to be going away from
the ocean and back toward the fountain.
It is not so far toward the ocean as another
drop which is hurrying by it with its eager
face set toward the sea; and yet the back-
ward-plunging drop will reach the ocean
first. The drop which now is hurrying
seaward will have the same weary circuit
to make before it can really find the sea it
seeks. It is a blessed thing to know that
both of them, in all their eddyings and
wanderings, are borne upon the bosom of
a stream greater than either of them, which
never ceases to press onward to the ocean
which is the final home of all.

There is no law which it is more necessary for one who studies human life and
character to understand, than this law to
which I have just alluded. The "law of the
three conditions" we may call it. The law
of life, death, and the higher life would
be its fuller name. Jesus said, "Except a
man be born again, he cannot see the
kingdom of God." "Whosoever loseth his

life for My sake," he said, "the same shall save it." See what some of the illustrations are. The crude hopefulness of boyhood passes through the disappointments which it is sure to meet, and comes out, if it keeps its health, into the robust and sanguine faith of middle age. A merely traditional religion goes into doubt, and gathers there strength of personal conviction, and comes forth the reasonable religion of a full-grown man. Innocence perishes in temptation, to be born again out of the fires as virtue. Life, death, and resurrection is the law of life; and bigotry and tolerance can never be deeply understood unless we know how easy indulgence often has to die in narrow positive conviction before it can be born again as the generous tolerance of the thoroughly believing man.

The truth that qualities have their qualities, is one which we need always to remember. You have not told the whole story when you have said that a man is kind, or brave, or truthful, any more than you have given a complete account when you have said of the sunset or of the bird's wing that it is red, when you have said of the sky or of the violet that it is blue. As there are colors of colors, so there are qualities of qualities. "*How* is he truthful, or brave, or kind?" That question still remains for you to ask. And in large part this quality of a quality will be indicated by the motive which at any particular moment calls the quality forth into action. The qualities of qualities are largely denoted by the colors of their motives shining through. This is quite true of tolerance. Let me enumerate very briefly some of the qualities of that quality, and see how each one is colored by the hue of its motive. I think that in various kinds of tolerance we can see six colors distinctly shining through. First, there is the lowest of all, that of which I have already spoken,—the tolerance of pure indifference, the mere result of aimless good-nature. If

I do not care, or do not think it possible to know, whether there is a God or not, why should I not be perfectly willing that this man should say that there is, and this other man should say that there is not? Secondly, there is the tolerance of policy, — the allowing of error because it would do more harm than good to try to root it out, the voluntary disuse of a right to eradicate it, the leaving of the tares for the wheat's sake. This is the tolerance of which Burke speaks when he says that " Toleration is a part of moral and political prudence." Thirdly, there is the tolerance of helplessness. This is the acquiescence in the utterance of error because we cannot help ourselves. It is the tolerance of persecuted minorities. It was the tolerance of Jeremy Taylor, writing the " Liberty of Prophesying " while the Parliament were masters in the land. Fourthly, there is the tolerance of pure respect for man. In entire disagreement with a man's opinion, you are able still cordially to recognize his right to his own thought, simply because he is a man, whether his thought will do harm or good. Fifthly, there is the tolerance of spiritual sympathy. The man's opinions are all wrong; but he means well, and you have grown to feel the value of your spiritual oneness. And sixthly, there is the tolerance of the enlarged view of truth, combined with a cordial and entire faith in God. This is the tolerance for which Milton has pleaded in his application of the myth of Typhon and Osiris, — the tolerance which grows up in any man who is aware that truth is larger than his conception of it, and that what seem to be other men's errors must often be other parts of the truth of which he has only a portion, and that truth is God's child, and the fortunes of truth are God's care as well as his.

These are the six, — indifference, policy, helplessness, human respect, spiritual sympathy, the vastness of God's truth. These are the different colors which may shine

through men's tolerances and show what
is the quality of this quality in each of
them. You see where the group divides,
— in the middle. The first three kinds of
tolerance have something base about them;
the last three are all noble. Just where
that cleavage and division runs, the death
of tolerance of which I spoke a while ago,
is very likely to come in. Just there, a
man entering into the power of some
strong conviction is liable to become intolerant; and his intolerance, coming there
and thus, is full of hope for the better tolerance which lies in its three degrees beyond. The man is at sea only because he
has set sail from the solid shore which is
malarious and barren, to reach by and by
the far more solid land which is bright and
healthy and fruitful. Do you not see how
necessary it is to know the kind of a man's
tolerance, to see what is the quality of this
quality in every tolerant man?

If we try to get still deeper at the roots
of the impression which prevails so widely,

that positive convictions are unnecessary to, and even incompatible with, the tolerance of opinions which are different from our own, I think that we shall find that it results from the low and meagre idea which so many people, even of those who talk the most about the sacredness of their convictions, have with regard to what a real conviction is. A true conviction, anything thoroughly believed, is personal. It becomes part of the believer's character as well as a possession of his brain; it makes him another and a deeper man. And every deepening of a human nature centralizes it, so to speak; carries it in, that is, to the centre of the sphere upon whose surface are described all the specific faiths of men. At the centre of that sphere sits the Spirit of Truth, of which all these specific faiths of men are the more or less imperfect and distorted utterances. The man who comes into that central place sits there with the Spirit of Truth and feels her power going out to the

faiths she feeds on every side. It is in
virtue of that centralness which he has
reached that he is able to understand and
sympathize with the whole. Deepen the
Desert of Sahara to the centre of the earth,
and it will know how the Himalayas came
to be so rocky and so high. And so the
advice to give to every bigot whom you
want to make a tolerant man must be, not,
" Hold your faith more lightly, and make
less of it;" but, " Hold your faith more
profoundly, and make more of it. Get
down to its first spiritual meaning; grasp
its fundamental truth. So you will be glad
that your brother starts from that same
centre, though he strikes the circumference at quite another point from yours."
It is true, strange as it sounds at first, that
the more deeply and spiritually a man
believes in fixed endless punishment of
wicked men, the more, and not the less,
tolerant he will become of his brother who
cherishes the eternal hope.

Perhaps it is stating the same truth in a

little different way when we say that true
tolerance consists in the love of truth and
the love of man, each brought to its perfection and living in perfect harmony with
one another; but that these two great affec-
tions are perfect and in perfect harmony
only when they are orbed and enfolded
in the yet greater affection of the love
of God. The love of truth alone grows
cruel. It has no pity for man. It cries
out, "What matter is a human life tortured
or killed for Truth, crushed under the
chariot-wheels with which she travels to
her kingdom?" The stake-fires and the
scaffolds belong to it. And the love of
man alone grows weak. It trims and
moulds and travesties the truth to suit
men's whims. "Do you want truth to be
this? Then this it shall be," it cries to
the faithless or the lazy soul. The boy of
whom the stranger asked the way to Farm-
ington is the very image of the love of
man that is not mingled and harmonized
with love for truth. "It is eight miles,"

the boy replied. "Are you sure that it is
so far as that?" the weary traveller asked.
The boy, with his big heart overrunning
with the milk of human kindness, looked at
him and replied, "Well, seeing you are
pretty tired, I will call it seven miles."
How much of would-be tolerance has
sounded in our ears like that! The love
of truth alone is cruel; the love of man
alone is weak and sentimental. It is only
when truth and man are loved within the
love of God, loved for His sake, truth
loved as His utterance, man loved as His
child, — only then is it that they meet and
blend in tolerance. Therefore it is that
absolute and steadfast tolerance, so far
from being the enemy of religion, as men
have foolishly said, can only come relig-
iously, can never be complete till man
completely loves his God.

May I not turn, as I speak, and ask the
personal experience of the thoughtful students who hear me to bear witness to the
truth of what I have said? Has it not

been true with you, that the more sure you have been, the more tolerant you have been always? Why is it that we are often so much more ready to tolerate those who differ from us by the entire heaven, than those whose different light twinkles close by our side in the same constellation? We have full tolerance for the Buddhist and the Mohammedan; less for the Quaker and the Congregationalist; least of all for the man of our own Church, but of another " school of thought" from ours. " The conforming to ceremony hath been more exacted than the conforming to Christianity," declared Lord Falkland of the Government of his day in a speech in the Parliament of 1640. Does it not all mean that where the difference is greatest, we are most sure of our ground, and so most tolerant? Where the difference is least, we have most misgivings, and there tolerance is weak. Does it not all witness to the truth of our doctrine that the best tolerance demands assured and settled faith?

Perhaps it is not desirable, certainly it is not possible, in the short space which I can give to that portion of my subject, to undertake anything like a detailed history of the growth of the spirit of tolerance among mankind. I only say in passing that there are few subjects so interesting and important which have been so inadequately treated. There is no worthy book upon the subject. To write one might well be the satisfaction and honor of any man's life. All that I undertake to do in this direction now is just to indicate some points in the history of tolerance which seem to illustrate the principles of tolerance which I have been trying to describe, confining myself entirely to that part of the history of tolerance which lies within the region of the Christian Faith.

The Jews were intolerant deliberately and on purpose. It was the other side of human progress which was being moved forward in their history. They were appointed to learn and manifest the power

of positive belief. Their history is like the
hard, tight stalk of a plant which is built
compactly and exclusively, just in order
that it may minister to a great radiant,
generous flower which is to bloom upon
its summit. That flower came in Christ;
and there in Him was set clearly and perfectly before the world the pattern of the
consummate tolerance. The love of truth
and the love of man, each complete and
each in perfect harmony with the other,
within the embracing love of God, — is not
that the life of Jesus? Not for a moment
does one doubt His absolute hold on
truth; it is so deep that He not merely
holds the truth, He is the truth. And
yet His patient, willing indulgence of His
brethren, His utter refusal to use any power
except reason and spiritual persuasion to
turn them from their error, — all this is
just as clear as His belief; and in Him
there can be no doubt that the two essentially belong together.

With this high, clear note struck, with

this image and pattern burning before her
for her guidance, the Church started on
the long, slow struggle to attain the same
high tolerance, to match the pattern of
her Master with her obedient life. In the
Apostolic Church and that which immediately followed it, the spirit of tolerance
was kept in a remarkable degree. Here
and there, no doubt, we see the signs of
a crowding forward on the side of intolerant positive belief; but the spirit of
brotherly kindness was so strong that almost immediately the other side, the side
of tolerant indulgence, was brought up to
meet it. And then, in those earliest days,
the Church was persecuted; and persecution always makes the persecuted man or
church a champion of tolerance.

With the cessation of persecution, with
the establishment of Christianity under
Constantine, came, in the midst of many
other evils, the enthronement and domin-
ion of intolerance. The persecution of
Jews, of pagans, and of heretics, thence-

forth became accepted. The love of truth, as men interpreted it, had cast away the love of man, and the reason lay in the abandonment or the corruption of the love of God.

Like so many other practices and dispositions of mankind, Saint Augustine took the disposition of intolerance and backed it with theory and established it into a principle. Indeed, the life of Augustine illustrates within itself much of what we have said upon our subject. As he became more earnest, he became less tolerant. These are his words in his earlier days: "Be not offended at seeing among yourselves sinners, and even heretics. What know you of their future state? Nay, more, what know you of their present state in the mind of God?" And these are his words much later in his fervid and eager life: "I abandoned my first opinion, overcome not so much by the reason of those who opposed it, as by the examples which they set before my

eyes. They showed me my own city of
Hippo, which, after having belonged wholly
to the Donatists, was converted and re-
united to the Catholic Church by the fear
of the imperial laws, and which has now
such a horror for that unhappy schism
that you could not believe that it had ever
been engaged in it." That method of conversion " by the fear of the imperial laws "
the great African bishop left firmly established in the Christian Church.

And so it remained through all the
Middle Ages, with only occasional out-
breaks of local and individual remon-
strance. It hardened into dogma, as at
the first Lateran Council. It blazed out
in fury, as when De Montfort slaughtered
the Albigenses in 1209. It struck its roots
deep as an institution when Innocent the
Third established the Inquisition in 1208.
The cloud broke open for a moment and
let a ray of sunlight through, as in the
teaching of a great, generous-hearted man
like Saint Bernard. There were pauses

in the dreadful history of persecution because there were times of absolute con-
formity, when there were no heretics to
persecute; but the whole dark tenor of
the mediæval history is really one and
the same. It is what Saint Thomas
Aquinas wrote with such fearful, calm
deliberation and such blankly fallacious
reasoning: "If the corruptors of money,
and malefactors of other sorts, are at once
by secular princes justly given up to death,
much more may heretics, as soon as they
are convicted of their heresy, be not
merely excommunicated, but also justly
killed." That was the sum of mediæval
logic on the matter.

The Protestant Reformation brought
no sudden change of theory. The principle of persecution was asserted by many
of the Reformed Confessions; it was held
and declared by Luther, Calvin, Beza,
Knox, and even by Melanchthon, Cranmer,
and Ridley. "One mass," cried John
Knox, "is more fearful to me than if ten

thousand armed enemies were landed in
any part of the realm." But though the
theory remained, it was soon evident that
another spirit was at work within it. Men
of light stood up here and there, and, full
of the belief in positive truth, still pleaded
for tolerance. Of all the Reformers, in
this respect, Zwingli, who so often in the
days of darkness is the man of light, is
the noblest and clearest. At the confer-
ence in the Marburg he contrasts most
favorably with Luther in his willingness
to be reconciled for the good of the common cause; and he was one of the very
few who in those days believed that the
good and earnest heathen could be saved.
The same reaching after better light appears in more unlikely places. Even Calvin, when he gave up the proofs of the
heresy of Servetus, was moved to say that
it seemed to him that since he did not
wield the sword of Justice, it was his duty
to confute heresy by sound doctrine, rather
than to seek to extirpate it by any other

method; and Oliver Cromwell, who, after all, struck more nearly than any other Englishman of his time the true note of tolerance, wrote in his account of the storming of Bristol, which was read in all the congregations about London on the 21st of September, 1645 : " For, brethren, in things of the mind we look for no compulsion but that of light and reason."

These men were dogmatists, distinctly men of doctrine. It is a blessed thing that in all times, and never more richly than in the Reformation days, there have always been other men to whom religion has not presented itself as a system of doctrine, but as an elemental life in which the soul of man came into very direct and close communion with the soul of God. It is the mystics of every age who have done most to blend the love of truth and the love of man within the love of God, and so to keep alive or to restore a healthy tolerance. Indeed, the mystic spirit has been almost like a deep and quiet pool in which tolerance, when it has been growing old and weak, has been again and again sent back to bathe itself and to renew its youth and vigor. The German mystics of the fourteenth century made ready for the great enfranchisement of the fifteenth. The English Platonists, who had the mystic spirit very strongly, became almost the re-creators of tolerance in the English Church. The mysticism of to-day gives great hope for the earnest freedom of the future.

I must not try, interesting as the task might be, to enter into the vexed question of the tolerance or intolerance, or rather the mixture of tolerance and intolerance, in the men who brought the Christian religion to our American shores, and especially in the Puritans who came from England. Three things concerning them are worthy of our notice, — first, that the Puritans, who came direct from England, are always to be distinguished from the Pilgrims, who came by way of Holland and

caught some of the broader spirit of that
" nursery of freedom and good-will; " second, that the noblest utterance of hopeful
tolerance in all that noble century was in
the famous speech in which John Robinson,
their minister, bade loving farewell to his
departing flock at Leyden, in which occur
those memorable words: " I am verily
persuaded, I am very confident, that the
Lord has more truth yet to break out of
His holy Word; " and thirdly, that some-
where in the bitter heart of Puritanism was
hidden the power which, partly by development, and partly by reaction, was to
produce the freedom of these modern
days.

Confused, irregular, forever turning in-
side out, forever going back upon itself,
the history of Christianity, however super-
ficially we glance at it, seems to bear witness to three things, — first, that every
hard bigotry is always on the brink of
turning into tolerance, and every loose tolerance of hardening into bigotry; second,

that on the whole, positive belief and
tolerance are struggling toward a final harmony; and third, that true tolerance belongs with profound piety and earnest
spiritual life. In those three facts lie
wrapped up together the philosophy and
the hope of tolerance.

There is one other study in the history
of tolerance to which I should like to point
your thoughts, but which it would need at
least a whole lecture to follow out in anything like complete detail. In modern
times there are six books, five of them
proceeding from the English race, and the
other one having close connection with
and influence upon that English race, all
of them books of remarkable literary and
historical value, which, taken together, present the feeling of our race toward tolerance most picturesquely and correctly.
Let me recall to you their names, and
commend you to the study of them in
connection with each other.

Of these six books, three belong abso-

lutely to the seventeenth century, one
hovers between the seventeenth and the
eighteenth, one is most characteristically
of the eighteenth, and one is a nineteenth-
century book through and through.

The first, of course, is Milton's stately
work, the " Areopagitica, or the Speech
for the Liberty of Unlicenc'd Printing."
It was born of a special occasion in the
poet's life; but in it the noblest spirit
of his time finds utterance, as fire will
burst forth through any chink that offers.
Its style is like a king's robe, stiff with
embroidery of gold and jewels; but, as
always in Milton, the grandeur of language does not impair the clearness of the
thought. The book glows with the double
love of liberty and truth. Its argument is
in the first place for the reader's rights; in
the second place for the impossibility of
enforcing censorship; in the third place for
the incompetence of censors; and finally
for the dignity of the teacher. It is a
noble, all-embracing plea; and yet he

draws back from its last conclusions. " I
mean not tolerated popery and open super-
stition," he declares ; but when we are reading of the seventeenth century, we never
can forget that popery then was quite as
much a political as a religious question.

In 1644, the same year with Milton's
lofty work, there was put forth another,
which is to-day almost unknown. It wears
no king's robe, but rather the clumsy
gown of a Puritan saint. So quaint as to
be almost unreadable, full of forced con-
ceits, involved and confused in plan and language, Roger Williams's " Bloody Tenent
of Persecution for Cause of Conscience " is
yet perhaps the broadest and most unhes-
itating plea for tolerance in all its century.
It did great work, and excited fierce discussion in its time. John Cotton, of Bos-
ton, answered it, in the style of his day,
with " The Bloody Tenent of Persecution
washed and made white in the Blood of
the Lamb ; " to which the persecuted apos-
tle of Rhode Island answered with " The

Bloody Tenent yet more bloody by Mr.
Cotton's endeavor to wash it white." The
first book in the controversy is the only
valuable one of the series. It is a dia-
logue between Truth and Peace. Its language, its imagery, and the grounds of its
argument are Scriptural. Its protest is
that the armies of Truth, like the armies
of the Apocalypse, "must have no sword,
helmet, breastplate, shield, or horse but
what is spiritual and of a heavenly nature."
In that statement there is the sum of the
whole matter.

After the Puritan and the Heretic comes
the Churchman. Bishop Jeremy Taylor's
"Liberty of Prophesying" appeared in
1647. The music of the master of sen-
tences is still in the world's ears. The
service which he rendered to the simplicity
of truth can never be forgotten. His dem-
onstration of the futility of intolerance
leaves no room for dispute. And yet the
book has not the greatness of Milton's or
of Roger Williams's. It is the book of an

ecclesiastic. It deals rather with the impossibility of compulsion, as if, if it were possible, compulsion would not be so bad a thing. Its highest spirit is perhaps summed up in one sentence, in which it declares that " It is best every man be left in that liberty from which no man can justly take him unless he assure him from error." Here there is an alternative suggested ; although it is also suggested that that alternative is unlikely or impossible. But the very suggestion makes us less surprised to hear how at the Restoration the good bishop became at least a less ardent champion of tolerance than he had been in his days of exile and distress.

Coleridge has compared Milton's work with Taylor's, and has declared, with unnecessary harshness and insinuation, that " the man who in reading the two does not feel the contrast between the single-mindedness of the one, and the strabismus in the other, is — in the road to preferment." On the other hand, our own historian,

George Bancroft, has a glowing passage in which he makes comparison between Jeremy Taylor and Roger Williams. The latter he declares to be " the harbinger of Milton and the precursor and superior of Jeremy Taylor." "Taylor," he says, " limited his toleration to a few Christian sects; the wisdom of Williams compassed mankind." There is truth in what both Coleridge and Bancroft say; and yet the " Liberty of Prophesying" had a place which neither of the other books could have filled in English life and literature and religion.

The fourth of the great books of tolerance is Locke's " Letter of Toleration," which was published in 1689. By that time the spirit of the eighteenth century was already in the air, and the high ideal life of the earlier part of the seventeenth century had vanished. Locke belonged to the coming age, which he was doing more than any other Englishman to create; and his notion of tolerance is all characteristic of himself. It is of the

earth, earthy. It is all based on his con-
tract theory of government. He denies
altogether that the care of souls belongs
to the civil magistrate, because it has never
been committed to him. His book is to
Milton's, or Williams's, or Taylor's, what
the lawyer in the community is to the
poet, the philanthropist, or the priest.

The most powerful and the most characteristic book of tolerance of the eighteenth
century, Lessing's " Nathan the Wise," belongs not to England, but to Germany. Its
idea is that of the ring-story, which in it is
adapted from Boccaccio. Neither of the
three great religions, Jewish, Christian, or
Mohammedan, is exclusively or even pre-
eminently true. Every man born in one
of them should tarry in his birthplace. It
is in the truest sense a book of scepticism.
The truth which it discovers, the inspiration it imparts, are of the sceptic's kind.
It is the book which springs from and
which serves a transition time. It is a
book for the world to rest on for a moment,

and then almost immediately outgrow. The far less-known work of Lessing, his treatise on "The Education of the Human Race," is a much nobler book, and in its indirect and more unconscious way does greater work for tolerance.

And so, to come to our own age, there is no need to do more than name John Stuart Mill's "On Liberty" as the utterance of the true nineteenth-century voice on tolerance. It is utilitarian in a very high but a very distinct sense. The usefulness of tolerance; how both silenced truth and silenced error, and men who need truth, and the institutions of men which need men who have free access to discussion; how all of these will suffer if thought be enchained, — this is his argument. The usefulness of tolerance, — not directly its glory, its obligation, or its sacredness, — the usefulness of tolerance is what our prophet of the nineteenth century stands up to proclaim with his clear logic and strong style.

These are the six books. The first are greater than the last. The first three books strike a more lofty note and paint a purer color, because they define a higher motive of tolerance than the last three. This is because the seventeenth century is higher than the eighteenth, and because, after all, the best spirit of the nineteenth century is not really in its book on tolerance. Perhaps it is not in the tolerance of our time itself. Century of tolerance as ours is, we all know how much of the deepest spiritual life of our time, while it may have looked with no dislike upon the tolerant dispositions which were all about it, has not directly and enthusiastically lent them its inspiration.

And this leads me at once to what I want to say about the closing portion of my theme,—the hope of tolerance. I have spoken quite in vain unless you see how deeply I believe that the value of tolerance lies in its devoutness. I have tried to show not merely that a man may be cordially tolerant and yet be devoutly spiritual, but also that a man cannot attain to the highest tolerance without being devoutly spiritual. Too long have piety and tolerance seemed to be open foes, or to keep but an armed truce with one another. Too long have young thinkers on religion imagined that it was disloyal to the truth they held, and to the Master whom they loved, to strive after cordial sympathy with and understanding of the earnest men and systems who were farthest from their truth and from their Master. Here is the first hope for tolerance, — not for its wider extent, but for its better kind. It will grow more and more religious. It will be filled with deeper piety. We shall not in moral perplexity hope that a man may be tolerant in spite of his devoutness; we shall confidently expect a man to be tolerant because he is devout. The first duty, I think, of the young students of to-day, whose mature work lies in the future, is to adjust their minds to that expectation, and always to make themselves think of piety and tolerance, not as enemies, but as dear friends.

When the time comes in which that friendship of piety and tolerance shall be fully asserted and accepted, then will be written a greater book than any of those which have been dedicated to the praise of Freedom. Then the Milton or the Mill of that distant day, inspired with a yet more glowing love for liberty, feeling the power of a divine utilitarianism, will be able to describe tolerance so that it shall seem to be not, as it has so often seemed, the license of self-will or the refuge of despair, but the broadest and deepest obedience of the soul to Christ, and the full flower of the ripest piety of the most earnest sainthood. In such presentation of herself, which is her only true presentation, Tolerance must claim the heart of the world.

Until that day arrives it is our duty to strive that tolerance shall not be travestied and misdescribed either by bigotry on the one side, or by what is called "free thought" upon the other. Before all efforts for the extension of any principle or power must always come the effort to understand and to define it rightly; we must know what it is before we can be enthusiastic for it ourselves, or enthusiastically urge it on our fellow-men.

In all this long lecture I have not till now attempted to give a definition of tolerance. I have felt almost as one feels about life, — that he wants to live before he tries to tell himself or his brethren what life is; but now may we not say of tolerance that it is this: "The willing consent that other men should hold and express opinions with which we disagree, until they are convinced by reason that those opinions are untrue"? There are five things involved in that definition which I must beg you to notice. First, the consent is willing; it is no mere yielding of despair. It might have all the power to put down the error by force which pope or parliament ever possessed, and it would never

4

for a moment dream of using it. On the other hand, secondly, it is simply consent. Tolerance is not called upon to champion the cause in which it disbelieves, nor to lend trumpets through which what it believes to be error may be blown. For, thirdly, it is of the very essence of tolerance that there should be disagreement; and disagreement involves the positive conviction on which I have insisted all this evening. And, fourthly, the error which is not to be yielded until it is convinced of its untruth by reason, must be attacked by reason; and so the right and the duty of earnest discussion is included as a part of tolerance. And, fifthly, the tolerance which is patient toward what it counts honest error, is utterly impatient toward dishonesty, toward hypocrisy, toward self-conceit, toward cant, whether it be on the side of what the honest man thinks to be error, or of that which he thinks to be true. There is a moral intolerance which must go with intellectual tolerance to give it vigor.

Cordial, discriminating, positive, out-spoken, conscientious: all these things the perfect tolerance must be; all these things it is bound to be by its very definition.

Keeping these qualities, which must belong to the perfect tolerance, clearly in our minds, are there not certain things which we may say with regard to the way in which that perfect tolerance will some day or other come to be the established condition and the ruling power of the world?

1. I have already said, at most abundant length, that it cannot come about by mere indifference.

2. Equally sure is it that it cannot come by mere eclecticism. That is the dream that haunts some amiable minds. Some day, so such minds fancy, some great peace-maker will pick out from every system of thought its choicest dogma, and setting them together, will build a dogmatic home where every soul shall be completely satisfied, because when it looks up it will see its own chief article of faith set in a place

of honor in the walls. It will accept the dogmas of the other souls because of the light which they will get from this of its, and it will cease to mourn for the rest of its cherished possessions which have no place in the new structure, because of its thankfulness that this its principal treasure has been saved.

Of all the stories of eclecticism, I think that none is more interesting than that of the great Akbar, the mighty Mogul Emperor, him whom Max Müller calls " the first student of comparative religions." He lived and died almost three centuries ago; but his story reads like a record of life in one of the great cities of to-day. In his palace at Agra he held his Friday evenings, when Buddhist, Hindu, Mussulman, Sun-worshipper, Fire-worshipper, Jew, Jesuit, and Sceptic, all came and argued, and the great monarch sat and stirred the waters, and gathered out of the turmoil whatever pearl was anywhere cast up to the top. He did not exactly, like a modern lady of society, invite a college professor to lecture to her friends upon the Infinite, in her parlor, on a summer's afternoon; but he hung a Brahmin in a basket outside his chamber window, and bade him thence discourse to him of Brahma, Vishnu, Rama, and Krishna, till the great Akbar dropped asleep. The result was an eclectic faith, a state religion, a thing of shreds and patches, devised by the ingenious monarch, enforced by his authority, accepted by his obsequious courtiers, and dropping to pieces and perishing as soon as he was dead. It was the old first fatal difficulty of eclecticism, that each man wants to make his own selection, and no man can choose for others, but only for himself.

3. Nor is the promise of the future to be found in the idea that some day one of the present forms of faith, one of the present conceptions of God and man and life, shall so overwhelmingly assert its truth that every other form of faith shall come and

lay its claims before its feet and ask to be obliterated and absorbed. Truth has not anywhere been so monopolized. And no man who delights in the activity of the human mind as the first condition of the attainment of final truth by man, can think complacently of any period short of the perfect arrival at the goal of absolute certainty with reference to all knowledge, when man shall cease to wonder and cease to inquire, and so pass out of the possibility of error and mistake.

4. And yet, again, our hope cannot lie contentedly in the anticipation of a mere superficial unity of organization and of government which will cover over and make men forget the differences of thought and opinion which lie in their unreconciled diversity below. Great is the craving after unity, — so great, so deep, so universal, that we know it is a part of God's first purpose for humanity, and never can die out till it has found its satisfaction. But it is too great and

deep ever to find its final satisfaction
in identity of organization. You cannot
make the unit to be a unit by the exter-
nal unity of one hard shell. If the fruit
which you try to enclose is alive, it will
burst your shell to pieces as it grows. If
it be dead, your shell will soon hold only
a dry and rattling remnant, to which it
can give no life. No, the real unity of
Christendom is not to be found at last in
identity of organization, nor in identity of
dogma. Both of those have been dreamed
of, and have failed. But in the unity of
spiritual consecration to a common Lord
— so earnestly sought by every soul that,
though their apprehension of Him whom
they are seeking shall be as various as
are the lights into which a hundred jewels
break the self-same sunlight — the search
shall be so deep a fact, so much the deepest fact in every soul, that all the souls
shall be one with each other in virtue of
that simple fact, in virtue of that common reaching after Christ, that common

earnestness of loyalty to what they know
of Him. There is the only unity that
is thoroughly worthy either of God or
man.

That seems to many men, I know, to be
dim and vague. It is a terrible and sad
sign of how far our Christianity is from
its perfection that now, after these centuries of its sway, the central key and secret
of its power should seem dim and vague
to men. But the hope of the future,
the certainty of the future, is that the per-
sonality of Christ, as holding the loyalty
and love of all the varying orders of
mankind, and making them one in their
common affection and obedience to Him,
is to become more and more real with
every Christian generation, till it is at last
for all mankind, as it is now for multi-
tudes of earnest souls, the reallest thing in
all the world. Organizations and dogmas
are of aid as they help to that. When
that shall come, in the degree in which
that shall have come in any age, tolerance

will fill that age as it at last must fill the world with its great, active, thoughtful, stimulating, sympathetic peace.

It must follow from all this that tolerance is to come about, not by any transaction, not by compacts and bargains, not by deliberate concession and compromise, but by the rising flood of life. Its hope lies in the advancing spirituality of man. He who hopes for it, let him hope for it thus profoundly. He who fears it, let him take comfort in the assurance that it can never come except with such a deeper occupation of the life of man by God as shall rob it of all the dangers which he fears.

I turn to you, the students of theology, of God, of science, and of human life, — the future ministers of Christ. You must be men, you must be ministers, of tolerance. But the true way in which you can be that is to forget tolerance and be ever more and more completely men of truth and men of Christ. So you must

be led on into that only worthy tolerance
which, as I have tried to show to-night,
and as I should like to say once more before I close, consists of the love of truth
and the love of man harmonized and included in the love of God.

SECOND LECTURE.

THE second of the great Mogul emperors, the wise and energetic Jahangir, used to have a chain hung down from his citadel to the ground, communicating with a cluster of golden bells in his own chamber, so that every suitor might apprise the monarch of his demand for justice without the intervention of the courtiers. It would be interesting to know what the courtiers thought of such an apparatus. No doubt there were some to whom it was a great offence. Full of the thought of themselves, it seemed an insult and impertinence that any of his people should presume to approach their lord except through them. There must have been

other more generous natures who rejoiced
that, however irregularly, the direct and
fundamental relation between the monarch
and his people should be recognized, and
that the meanest man in all the kingdom
might send his complaint or his petition
direct to the king's ear. Doubtless also
there were those in whose breasts the
sight of the hanging chain wakened self-
questionings. Why was it that such an
apparatus was required? Why should
not these petitioners send their petitions
through the appointed channels? Had
the courtiers perhaps made their courtier-
ship too narrow and unsympathetic to be
the medium of interpretation between the
people and their lord?

All three of these suggestions come
into the mind of the Christian Church
when it sees human souls, apart from her
ordinances and institutions, seeking the
ear and heart of God. The first thought
springs up in the baser portion of the
Church's heart; the other two are good

and healthy. One of them is thankful that, valuable as the Church is to the soul and to the world, every son of God has still open to him that power of direct appeal and personal approach which the Church is meant to stimulate and help, but never to deny or supersede. The other thought keeps the Church full of wakefulness and watchfulness, ever on the alert to see how she can make herself less unworthy of her mission, a truer and broader minister of God to man. Both together preserve in the Church the spirit of tolerance.

May I not, as I begin to speak this evening to you, students of divinity, men who very soon will make a part of the Church's ministry, pause for a moment with a word of exhortation, and beg you never, in your thankfulness for all the Church's blessed richness, to forget the personal belonging of the child to the Father, of the human soul to God, which lies behind all that the Church can be or

do.   There will come times when in your
own deepest need or loftiest exaltation you
will forget that you are ministers, and
simply know yourselves as men, children
of God.   Then you will come directly to
Him heart to heart.   There are times
when the courtiers themselves, leaving the
whole courtly ceremonial aside, will touch
the chain and ring the golden bells.   Let
such moments interpret to you the simple,
personal, unchurchly religious impulses
which make up so much of the world's
religion.   Let such moments at once fill
you with a deep sense of the reality and
value of many a religious experience of
which the Church in her institutional life
takes no account, and let it also make you
anxious that the Church should be so simple
and true and human, so full of love and
faithfulness to human nature, that more
and more of the religious life of man may
find its ministry and help in her.   The
channel which is not wide enough to contain the full torrent of the spring-time is

thankful that the drops she cannot hold
find wayward courses of their own down
to the sea; and at the same time she
makes herself wider and wider, that more
and more of the water may find way
through her.

And now there are several subjects suggested by what I said the other evening
of which I should like to speak to you
to-night with more or less of order and
coherence. I said then, you remember,
that tolerance, so far from being a thing
of loose beliefs and feeble earnestness, had
its real life in certain convictions and profound piety. If this be so, then it is surely
true that the Church, which is the home of
clear faith and spiritual consecration, ought
to be the citadel of tolerance; and we, mem-
bers and ministers of the Church, ought
to look forward to the time when, setting
distinctly before the world the true nature
of this grace, she shall attract men by its
beauty and win men to it and to herself.

But now it is time for us to note a

distinction which has no doubt occurred to
a good many of your minds while I have
spoken. When we speak of tolerance, we
may have in our minds either one of two
classes of things and thoughts toward
which the tolerant disposition is de-
manded; and we may easily be led to
draw a line between them, and say:
" Toward one class tolerance is good;
but toward the other class, how is tolerance possible?" There is the tolerance
toward other forms of good thinking and
good working than our own; and there is
the tolerance toward forms of working and
thinking which we do not at all hold to be
good, but totally and irremediably bad.

The first thing which we can say with
regard to that distinction is, that it is one
of which we never ought to think that we
can be absolutely sure at first sight. Our
sense of the value of our way of working,
if it is very deep, — as it ought to be, in
order to make our work vital and enthusiastic, — is almost sure to blur the distinc-

tion between the work and the way of doing it, to make the color seem part of the substance, to make the man who is doing the same work in another way appear to be doing another work. Nowhere does a man need more clearness of mind and soul than here. The only thing that can keep him absolutely true is such a pure value for the thing itself, such a desire and craving for the success of the essential work, as shall compel it always to stand out before the thought sharp and distinguishable from all the ways in which the work is being done.

But granting that this distinction can be kept, then the objects for our tolerance fall into the two classes of which I spoke. First, there are the opinions which we recognize as probably or possibly presenting other sides of truth than ours. Here everything ought to be clear and easy, if we understand human nature. God has made man with two powers in relation to the laying hold on truth: one of these

5

powers is general, the other special. By
one of them man values truth in its essence, laying hold upon the fundamental
difference between truth and falsehood;
by the other, expressing itself in his peculiar faculties and character, he seizes upon
particular forms or kinds of truth and
makes them distinctively his own. The
true student is aware of both of these
powers, and never lets them lose themselves in one another. " I love truth," he
says, sweeping into the range of his affection all the unknown truth that every special scholar is discovering in the most
distant regions of investigation. What the
astronomer is seeing in the skies, and the
mathematician in the mystery of form and
number, and the metaphysician in the soul
of man, — all these the truth-lover claims
for his own as he stands at the heart of
things and says, " I love truth." And yet
this does not hinder him from putting
forth his special faculty and comprehend-
ing, as we say, one special kind of truth,

and enthusiastically declaring, " This is my truth." This double hold on truth is all-important. If the first element is lost, the scholar narrows to a meagre special- ist; if the second element grows weak, he fades into a vague and abstract theorist. He must have both. But he is very sure not to have both; he is very sure to lose the larger hold on truth in its essence, — truth as truth, — unless he knows, and is rejoiced to know, that other men are holding other truths than his; and what we are used to call other sides of truth are really other truths. It is very like our conception of the world we live in. I love my country, and I love the whole earth; but my love for the total earth would fade and grow dim if I did not realize and re- joice that men with my humanity were liv- ing at the Tropics and at Baffin's Bay. It is in virtue of my being at once an Ameri- can and a man that my intelligence and my love can take possession of the world.

Therefore no man is truly tolerant who

does not merely consent, but rejoice that other men think differently from himself regarding those subjects of thought which are capable of various apprehension. I have heard some of our bishops declare with thankfulness and pride that there was no difference of opinion in their dioceses; that all the clergy (I suppose they would hardly undertake to answer for all the laity there) thought alike. I know some ministers who want all their parishioners to think after their fashion, and are troubled when any of their people show signs of thinking for themselves and holding ideas which the minister does not hold. Thank God, the human nature is too vital, especially when it is inspired with such a vital force as Christian faith, to yield itself to such unworthy slavery. Many and many is the minister who, when his people have first gone forth, full of the fire which God has sent to them through him, to think of God as he taught them to think of Him, has by and by become a learner from his people's lives, and found in their experience how good it is that the divine light shines on many mirrors and completes its revelation in no single soul!

Of the other class of things of which I spoke, the case is different. I am not called upon, nay, I am not at liberty, to rejoice in the existence of any opinion which I know to be untrue. I am not called upon, nay, I have no right, to be thankful that my neighbor is an atheist, and denies the truth of God's being, which is to me the glory and the inspiration of all life. Tolerance toward him means something different from a glad sense that he fills out my partial truth with something which it lacked. Tolerance toward him means two things. It means, first, a cordial and thankful recognition of all the good personal character which there is in him, including most carefully the frankness and honesty which makes him clearly face and openly declare this very atheism which distresses and offends my soul. It means, in the second

place, the full acceptance of the idea that
it is only by the persuasion of reason that
this atheism can be legitimately attacked
and overthrown.   Where these two elements, personal respect and confidence in
reason only as the means of conversion,
are present, tolerance is perfect.   Then the
strong platform is built on which you can
meet your atheist or unbeliever and wage
strong warfare for the truth which you
believe.   Upon that platform let no earnestness be spared.   One of the worst things
about intolerance is that its puts an end to
manly controversy.   Calvin cannot argue
with Servetus when he is putting the fire
to the fuel which surrounds his victim at
the stake.   Laud cannot demonstrate epis-
copacy to the Puritans whom he despises
and believes that it is right to put down
by force.   The only atmosphere in which
strong, manly controversy, which is one of
the noblest activities on earth, can truly live
and flourish, is the atmosphere of tolerance, — an atmosphere whose elements are

respect for personal qualities and trust in the power of truth.

All this applies especially to that which often seems to be the hardest kind of tolerance, which is the tolerance of intolerance. Very often this is the last infirmity of liberal minds. After you have conquered or outgrown all your unwillingness that men should think in enterprising and dangerous ways, you turn and look in on yourself, only to find your soul full of uncharitable thoughts towards men who still are keeping the reluctance which you used to feel. Until you get rid of those thoughts you are not fully tolerant. It is possible to get rid of them. Towards the narrow-minded bigot both of the dispositions of which I spoke may come into full play. You may feel in his bigotry the high quality of personal sincerity, and you may cordially own that not even so unpleasant a usurper as his bigotry must be attacked with any other artillery but reason. So you may be tolerant even of intolerance, — which is very hard.

2. I pass on, next, to speak of the way in which the question of tolerance is related to the declared and visible fellowships of men. It may be that what I have said thus far has seemed too large. Intolerance, as it exists to-day, does not, consciously and declaredly, at least, seek to banish from existence those with whom it disagrees. It says only that it cannot include them in the group of privileged men, in the community, the society, the church which holds only those who think aright. Let us look at this for a few moments.

We must remember, then, that there is more than one fellowship which must be taken into account in estimating a man's relation to his fellow-men. Every true Churchman, — that is, every man who truly values his place in the Christian Church, — it seems to me, must think of himself as standing in the midst of four concentric circles. He is the centre of them all. They represent the different groups of his

fellow-men with whom he has to do. They
sweep in widening circumference around the
spot of earth on which he stands, and make
the different horizons of his life. What
are they? Outermost of all, there is the
broad circle of humanity. All men, simply
as men, are something to this man. It is
the consciousness " Homo sum," the consciousness which the Latin poet crowded
into his immortal line, which fills this circle
with vitality. Next within this lies the
circle of religion, — smaller than the other,
because all men are not religious, but large
enough to include all those of every name,
of every creed, who count their life the subject and the care of a Divine life which is
their king. Next within this lies the circle
of Christianity, including all those who,
under any conception of Him and of their
duty toward Him, honestly own for their
Master Jesus Christ. And then, inmost of
all, there is the circle of the man's own
peculiar Church, the group of those whose
thought and worship is in general identical

with his who stands in the centre and feels all these four circles surrounding him.

Can you not seem to see him standing there in the midst of these circumferences? And the first thing of importance is that each one of the four should be real to their central man, and never wholly lost out of his consciousness. It will not do for either of them to become unreal; all the others will surely suffer if it does. To the true disciple, to the real member of the Church of Christ, it must still be a fact of which he is aware, and which he thinks most important, that he belongs with other Christians who think of Christ differently from himself, and with religious men who never heard of Christ, and with all men simply in virtue of their being men, whether they are religious men or not.

Of course the relationships with all these groups are different. The four radii of the four circles vary very much in length. The inmost circle nestles to its centre with a warmth of sympathy which the others do not know. That is all right. But the important point is that they all are real. There come times in the life of the member of Christ's Church when he needs each one of these four horizons of life, — times when the close foreground of completest sympathy is what his soul requires; times when the middle distance of a more general unity of faith, a unity with those who own and love the same Christ differently conceived, or with those whose souls are touched with the same great general aspirations in some pagan faith, enlarges his view of the presence of God in the world; still other times, when nothing short of the great mountain-tops of humanity which stand around all special human living and thinking will satisfy his gaze.

I value very much this doctrine of the concentric circles, this doctrine of the four horizons, because I think that in forgetfulness of it lies the secret of many of the corruptions of the Church's faith and life. The " unity of faith ! " we say. Of course

those words have their most close and
sacred meaning, as they express the deep
sympathy of men who in almost all points
of belief see eye to eye, and perfectly
agree, — men who delight in the common
service of a Master whom they understand
alike. But that inmost unity of faith grows
weak and narrow unless the men who feel
it feel also constantly the unities of faith
which lie beyond. I cannot live truly with
the men of my own Church unless I also
have a consciousness of common life with
all Christian believers, with all religious
men, with all mankind.

And then we note another thing: not
merely are these four circles all real to the
true Churchman, — the circles of humanity, of religion, of Christianity, and of his
Church; they also feel each other, and the
inner and smaller are always reaching out-
ward to the larger. The Churchman as he
lives in all of them becomes aware that,
actually distinct as they are now, they are
ideally and essentially identical with one

another. He feels a throb and thrill through all the system, which he finds to be the effort of the smaller circle to embrace the larger. Each smaller circle is restless and discontented until it at least has touched the larger circumference of which it always is aware. The special Church reaches out and craves to enlarge itself until it shall be able to include within itself all Christianity. Christianity is anxious to claim all the religious life of all the world for Christ; and true religion grows more and more anxious to declare that religion is not something foreign to humanity, that it is simply the fullest utterance of human life, that all human life which is not religious falls below itself. Not man with religion is something more, but man without religion is something less, than man.

Most interesting is this perpetual outreach, this throb and struggle of the inner circles to fill the outer circles with themselves. But it touches our present purpose only so far as it describes the relation between the inmost circle and the one that lies next beyond it, — the circle of the Church and the circle of general Christianity. There it touches directly upon most important questions, — upon questions which you, young clergymen, will have to meet almost as soon as you find yourselves ordained. The Church horizon, as I said, is always reaching out toward the Christian horizon and trying to identify itself with it. If it could perfectly do so, all would be well. But there is not a Church in Christendom which can do so to-day. There is not a Church in Christendom — not ours, nor any other — which is not forced to own that there are men whom she will freely acknowledge to be Christian men, whom yet she is not ready and fit to receive into full communion and membership with herself, into full acceptance of her privileges and full enjoyment of her influence. Some dogma doubted, or some dogma held, or some peculiarity of thought or feeling on their part, stands in the way. Some excess or some defect of faith keeps the Christian outside the Christian Church!

Is it not so? I can see nothing to do but frankly to face the fact and own it. A man comes to you, who are a minister of our Church, and tells you of his faith, tells you how earnestly he loves, how deeply he honors, the Lord Jesus Christ, tells you how he is trying to give his whole life up to the Master's service. Is he a Christian? Of course he is; you cannot doubt a moment. You are sure what the Lord would have said if He had met him in Jerusalem. But can you, simply and solely because he is a Christian, throw wide the door and bid him welcome to our Church's inmost privileges? Are there no tests of doctrine, no specified ways of worship, no definitions of orthodoxy, which lie within the definitions of the absolute truth, which you must apply before you can bid that Christian welcome to the Church and feel that he

and it belong together? If there are,
then the Church is not prepared to-day
to make herself identical with Christianity. If the chance to do so were freely
given her, she is not ready to accept it.
Therefore she is not catholic; she is not
prepared to lay claim to universality.

And what must be the consequence of
such a state of things? Must there not
be two consequences? The first consequence must be a perpetual restlessness
under her own restraint, a perpetual desire to make all thought orthodox which
is true, and all action legitimate which is
really helpful to the human soul. We
ought to be very thankful for every such
disposition wherever it shows itself in our
Church. We ought to be very glad when,
reaching out in either way, — either back
into the past, gathering up any disused
method which the Church may have now
grown wise enough to use; or forward
into the future, eagerly claiming any light
which free-minded criticism and enlarged

knowledge can throw upon the pages of the Bible, — the Church grows broader in spirit, more ready to do the work of God and to meet the religious needs of man.

The other consequence must be a cordial tolerance. So long as any Church is aware that there are Christians to whom she, as she is now constituted, cannot open her doors, she must be more than content — she must be thankful and rejoice — that there are forms of worship and groups of believers in which those Christians for whom she has no place may find fellowship with one another and feed their souls with truth. While she is ever trying to make her own embrace more large, to bring herself into a true identity with the absolute Christianity, she will be glad enough that in the mean time the souls for which she has no place are not to go unhoused, that there are other Church homes than her own in which they may live, that she is not the whole Church, that in the largest and truest

sense the Church, even to-day, does embrace all servants of Christ in their innumerable divisions. Such souls there must
be so long as there is no Church in the
world which is exactly coincident with
essential Christianity, no Church which
makes the standards of her membership
exactly the same, — not one whit more, as
well as not one whit less than the standard
by which a man would have a right to
count himself and to think that Christ
would count him a true servant of the
Lord of Christians. If there are two circles, one less than the other, those who live
in the space between the two must be ac-
counted for. This is the ground on which
the man and the minister who believes
most enthusiastically in his own Church
may yet keep — nay, must yet keep —
a true tolerance for other churches.

The great safeguard and assurance of
the tolerant spirit in the Christian minister
then lies in the clear distinctness of these
four horizons about the central point on

which he stands. He does not stand related to them all alike; one presses more
closely than another on his life. But to
know that he has relations to them all, and
to keep those relations distinct and true,
that is his safety. First, and most cen-
trally, he is a man of his own Church.
Her doctrines he believes, her methods he
devoutly uses, her history he studies. By
her peculiar genius his life is colored and
inspired. He never dreams of anything
but loyalty to her. But he goes out beyond her in his interest and study, and
tries sympathetically to understand all that
the Christian workers are doing, all that
the Christian thinkers and scholars are discovering, in any of the rich fields in which
they work. He is a Christian, and nothing
done or thought in the name of Christ is
foreign or alien to him. Then he goes
out to a still wider circle. All that the
religious life of the world before Christ
and aside from Christ has been and has
accomplished, is of interest to this man

standing in his central Church. Not in
supercilious pity, not in a spirit of cap-
tiousness which tries only to see their
weaknesses and faults, but with a profound reverence for them all as true reve-
lations of his own beloved God, as faint
shinings through the cloud of his own en-
lightening Christ, so does the true Churchman study the religions of the ages
and of the world. He reveres in them the
God ever ready to show Himself to His
children, and the soul of man ever reaching forth, blindly, awkwardly, stumblingly,
but with an irrepressible persistency to find
the Father. And then, last of all, man, —
all that he has been, all that he is, all that
he is making of this wonderful, beautiful
world; man with his history, his poetry,
his art, his science; man very often in his
deepest godlessness bearing most convinc-
ing witness of God by the way in which he
shows his need of Him — man in his simple
manhood makes the largest circle which
surrounds this central life.

Do you not see how every study in which it is possible for man to engage may be a true part of the minister's preparation for his work? Christianity in all its forms, comparative religion, human life, the world he lives in, all these he must know in some degree, in as great degree as is in his power. Is he not the most central man in all the world? Must he not be inspired and filled with devoutness, vitality, and tolerance as he stands in the midst of his horizons?

3. Let me pass to another topic. The question of tolerance will probably always be connected with the question of penalty. Not that they are necessarily connected; it is possible for a man to be intolerant of an opinion different from his own, and yet never to feel that he has a right to assign a penalty to the holding of that opinion, or even to want to say what will befall the man who holds it. Penalty is the shadow which condemnation casts when it shines down smitingly upon the thing which it condemns. No doubt sometimes the con-

demnation may take place in such a clear, diffused light of pure thought that it may cast no shadow.   The intolerant man may be content to say, " I hold that opinion to be wholly base and wrong and mischievous, and I would put it down even by force if I could," and yet may not be tempted on to denounce punishment upon the man who believes that opinion to be true.   I do not doubt that there is a great deal of such intolerance as that.   Many people are ready to believe that with the passing away of the use of axe and fagot in religious persecution all pronouncing of penalty in religious differences has disap- peared.   I wish that it were so.   The evil of intolerance would be vastly less if it simply denounced and upbraided the opin- ion with which it disagreed, and did not go farther, and condemn it to a punishment, the fear of which once attached to any opinion is a most serious obstacle to the discovery of the degree of truth which that opinion may contain.

" But," people say, " how is this possible? Now that we cannot burn our
heretics, and now that they do not mind
our excommunications, how can there be
such a thing as persecution any more? "
I answer, " If it be possible to keep alive
the idea — if in some of her teachings the
Church does keep alive the idea — that
wrong opinions about God and Christ and
salvation are not merely to show their
influence in hampered and harmed lives,
but are also to be definitely punished by
God as wickedness, then the most terrible form of persecution is still possible."
People used to shut out a certain doctrine
from the reach of fair inquiry by decreeing
that whoever came to believe that doctrine
should be stretched upon the rack, and
then be led through the hooting streets in
a disgraceful dress, and at last burned with
fire in the public square. What terror had
a penalty like that compared with the
terror which belongs to this other threat,
which declares or implies that he who

believes this or disbelieves that shall per-
ish everlastingly? Can such a declaration
still let the soul be free to seek for truth?
Must it not make very difficult, if not impossible, that search after the truth mixed
and hidden in the error which ought to be
our strongest desire when we deal with
things which we esteem erroneous?

I cannot doubt that the present confused
and rebellious condition of men's minds
with regard to the punishments of the
future life comes in part, and in large part,
from the way in which punishment in all
ages of the Church has been denounced
upon speculative opinions and earnest convictions. Bidden to believe that souls
would be punished for wrong-thinking,
people have come to doubt whether souls
would be punished for anything at all.
The only possibility of any light upon the
darkness, any order in the confusion, must
lie in the clear and unqualified assertion
that such as God is can punish such as
men are for nothing except wickedness,

and that honestly mistaken opinions are not wicked. How a clear assertion of such a simple truth as that cuts the knot of sophistry at once; how it makes the whole system of persecution for opinion's sake appear impossible! It would have seemed as if that simple truth were quite self-evident. But it is not. The whole long, awful history of persecution and torture for opinion's sake proves that it is not. A multitude of men to-day have abandoned the idea of persecuting their brethren for their opinions, only because they either, on the one hand, have seen the hopelessness and uselessness of it, or else, upon the other hand, have been willing to leave the punishment of the errorist to God. That sort of tolerance is superficial and unstable. The only ground for us to take is simply the broad ground that error is not punishable at all. Error is not guilt. The guilt of error is the fallacy and fiction which has haunted good men's minds. It has not always stood out plain and clear; such fictions seldom do. It has been mixed with thoughts of the mischievousness of error, and with suspicions of the maliciousness of error; but always lying in behind, in the centre of the impulse which made man persecute his brother man for what he thought, there has been the idea that error was guilt. We must get rid of that entirely. Error is not like guilt; error is like disease. Behind disease there may lie guilt as a cause, — the man may have been wicked, and so made himself sick; and so a man may have been reckless, defiant, sophistical, selfish, wicked in many ways, and so have plunged himself into error. But he may have fallen into error without any such wickedness; and even if his error be the fruit of wickedness, it is in the wickedness, the moral wrong, and not in the error which has proceeded from it, that the guilt lies.

Guilt could be inseparably attached to error only on the assumption that there was on earth some revelation of God's truth so absolutely sure and clear that no honest man could possibly mistake it, — so sure and clear that any man who mistook it must necessarily be wanton and obstinate and disobedient; and such a revelation certainly does not exist, and never has existed on the earth.

The most striking indications, to my mind, that error is not guilt, and does not properly call forth those emotions which only guilt ought to produce, lies in the way in which many opponents of error feel called on to ascribe base motives to the men who hold it. They have to turn error into moral wrong before they can abuse it as only moral wrong deserves to be abused. They are like the Inquisitors of old, who when they led their victims to the stake, dressed them in grotesque and horrid garments that the populace along the street might forget that they were men, and hoot at them with free voices and consciences as if they were fiends. When a controversialist, arguing against a certain doctrine which he thinks all wrong, charges its upholders with "the subtlety of the adulterer and the cold-blooded cruelty of the assassin," have we not a clear token of misgiving; have we not a sign that he himself believes that not in pure error, but only in malignant dispositions found or feigned in errorists, is their real guilt or the real ground of moral reprobation of their thinking?

Once get rid of the whole notion that error is in itself a guilty thing, and two good results must follow, — first, moral indignation, called back from the false scent on which it has been wasting itself, will have its time and strength to give to those things which are really worthy of its hatred. Again and again in history the Church, pursuing error with her anathemas, has forgotten to denounce cruelty, hypocrisy, and corruption, which were flagrant in her very bosom. Blame given to the blameless makes us very often most lenient to the blameworthy. Insincerity (whether it profess to hold what we think is false or what we think is true), cant, selfishness, deception of one's self or of other people, cruelty, prejudice, — these are the things with which the Church ought to be a great deal more angry than she is. The anger which she is ready to expend upon the misbeliever ought to be poured out on these.

And, again, when the denouncing of penalties on wrong belief shall be done with, then the calm portrayal of the consequences of wrong belief shall have a better chance. To tell an honest unbeliever that God will punish him for not believing that which his mind can see no sufficient reason for accepting, — that, if he is a real man, only fixes him more certainly in unbelief. To point out to him how his unbelief is shutting him out of great regions of joy and growth, and robbing his nature and separating him from God, — that is legitimate enough.

It cannot make him believe, — only positive evidence ought to do that, — but it
can set him to a more serious examination
of evidence, and take away from the truth
that air of unlikelihood which is the atmosphere in which so many of the wanderers
go astray.

In all our thinking and speaking we are
to stand guard over the purity of ideas.
And the wrong use, the wrong application,
of an idea violates and vitiates its purity;
so that when it comes back to its true
application, it works feebly or works
falsely.   It is as if you whittled your fire-
wood with the surgeon's knife; when the
next delicate operation comes, the fine-
ness and the sharpness are not there.
You love an unlovely nature, and your
very power of love grows coarse; when
the true loveliness stands up before you,
your love is coarse and lustful.   You ad-
mire baseness, and you have nothing but
a debased admiration to give to nobleness.
You hate a troublesome truth, and it is

only a weak and peevish dislike, not a generous indignation, which you have to bestow upon a flagrant lie. Like precious essences whose strength lies in their purity, are these capacities of strong emotion which make the worth and vigor of a human life.

Stand guard, then, over your moral condemnation ; do not let it go out against honest error. If you do, it will come back to you with its finest fire chilled and cooled, with its eager impetuosity hesitating and half palsied, with its reality dimmed and confused. Keep it till you meet a bad man, a false man, a cruel man. Then, just because you have not flung it out loose on all the errors which you dis-approved, but on which by its very nature it could take no hold, it will spring at the throat of the wickedness which by its very nature it was made to hate and is bound to try to kill wherever it can find it.

How quickly one discovers as one goes about in the strange, windy world of

protestants, reformers, radicals, philan-
thropists, and denouncers of the world's
innumerable wrongs, which are the few
among the multitude who have kept their
power of moral condemnation pure by
using it only at the right times and on
the right material. How they shine like
clear stars in the midst of the lurid light
of all the rest!

4. It is a truth which is essential to what I
have been saying, and one which for its own
great value cannot too often be repeated,
that the Christian faith is set on moral
ends and can find a satisfaction with which
it can be wholly satisfied only in human
character. This is a truth which affects
most fundamentally the priesthood of the
Christian minister. The purpose of the
Christian faith is man. Man is the end,
truth is the means. It is the place of
Christianity to take up the purposes of
God and keep the proportions of His
ways and standards. Christianity, then,
must hold man as her purpose, truth as

the means by which that purpose may be
reached; character always behind belief,
belief always as the gateway and vestibule
to character.

Now, the priest is the expression and
embodiment of Christianity; what the
Christian faith is in its great impersonal
abstractness, that he is in his active per-
sonality. He is the keeper of the things
of God. And of what things? Of truth,
no doubt. He is to find by every most
persistent search, to keep with sleepless
care the truth of God. If there is any
truth of God hidden in history or in the
methods of interpretation of the Sacred
Book, it is the priest's duty to go and find
it with the fearless search of consecrated
reason. Alas for him if he leave that
work to be done by unconsecrated and
perhaps by hostile hands! The keeper of
the truth of God, the priest is certainly;
but always for its purposes, always for
men. As God's great purpose on the
earth is man, not truth; as He will freely

7

let His truth be misunderstood, and wait in
perfect patience for the time when it can
free itself from misconceptions and come
out clear and sure, but will never let any
one of His children be put in a place where
he must necessarily do wrong, — so (and it
is the first truth of his ministry) the pri-
mary and final care of the true priest of
God is human character; and truth is in
his hands, not for its own value, but as an
instrument for that.

You, my friends, will be before many
years called to be priests in the Church of
God. With an ordination which you can
even now feel hovering over your heads,
you will find yourselves set apart to the
sacredest and most delightful life which
men can live. How shall you account of
yourselves? how shall you ask men to
account of you there? Paul says, "As
ministers of Christ and stewards of the
mysteries of God." A steward keeps his
treasures for their uses. He is no miser
or connoisseur, keeping his mysteries for

their own preciousness or curious beauty. The steward of the mysteries of God keeps truth for men; and back of his keeping of truth he keeps men, he keeps human character, he keeps the true qualities of the best humanity in the men committed to his charge, so that those qualities may not be lost or corrupted.

May this be your priesthood! May you count yourselves the keepers of truth; but may you count yourselves still more the keepers of truthfulness! May you dread a stain of error on the truth your people hold; but may you dread vastly more the stain of insincerity or self-deception in the way in which they hold any truth, however true! Great is the power of the priest who thus stands guard over the humanity of his people, and will not, if he can prevent it, let the most well-meaning adversary do it harm or dishonor. He has the most sacred of all the mysteries of God in charge; for a life is a more sacred mystery than any truth, and truth exists in the world but for the sake of human lives.

It is not strange in this world to see ends sacrificed to means; but it is no less sad because in history it has grown so familiar. I remember a curious illustration of it which I heard some years ago in England. It seems that in Westminster Abbey a good many Roman Catholics have been in the habit of coming, on the day of his sainthood, to pray beside the tomb of Edward the Confessor at the old shrine where petitions of devout pilgrims were offered up for centuries. The late Dean Stanley loved the custom; it pleased his catholicity and his historic sense, and he gave it all encouragement. But it seems that it did not so well please one of the old vergers or sextons of the Abbey; and one day when the worshippers were numerous, this venerable official came to one of them, and touching him on the shoulder as he knelt upon the ground, said: "You must go away from here."

The man meekly looked up and replied:
"Why? I am doing no harm." "No matter, you must go away," reiterated the
verger. "But why?" persisted the wor-
shipper, still on his knees. "I am doing
no harm; I am only praying." But the
verger persevered, and gave his most con-
clusive reason. "No matter, I tell you
you must go away; this thing must stop.
If this goes on we shall have people praying all over the Abbey!" There is a sort
of verger Churchman, more sexton than
priest of the house of God, who is always
for stopping free inquiry, because if this
thing goes on we shall have men seeking
for truth all over the Church of Christ.

The true priest knows that that is what
the Church of Christ is for, and welcomes
it; not merely for the truth which the
search will bring to the light, but for the
searcher's sake, he welcomes it. There
lies the real necessity that the priest
should be above all other things a man
with an intense and live humanity, thor-

oughly in sympathy with all that is best
and bravest and most vital in his fellow-
men. We all know how about the figure
of the priest in many of the centuries of
Christian history there has hung an air of
mystery and inhumanity. Men, women,
and priests have seemed to make up the
human race. The priest was separate from
all his fellow-men. He was the repository
of knowledge which nobody but himself
could understand. He lived by laws
which were different from those by which
other men must live. He ate strange
food, and wore strange clothes, and talked
in strange tones, and had power with men
because he was different from them. If
that was ever good, the day for it is past.
The priest to-day must stand in the centre
of all the four horizons and be the most
manly of all men. What it is good for
all men to be, he must be supremely;
what he is supremely, it must be good for
all other men to be. He must have the
widest sympathy, and preach by word

and life the broadest tolerance of all honest opinion, however various, however wrong. He must be the champion of the right of the most mistaken soul to hold and teach his opinion until he has become convinced that it is untrue; and at the same time he must be the pattern of intolerance upon the moral side, and have no patience with any sin, however respectable or useful. It is the fundamental conception of Christianity as a religion of character, and not of dogma, save as a means to character, which makes necessary and makes possible a priesthood such as this.

I have not left myself the space in which to speak as I intended of the detailed methods and means by which the minister of Christ may cultivate the broad and positive tolerance which I have praised in your hearing during these two lectures. But not to leave that subject totally untouched, I must say a few words about that power to which many

people in these days are looking as the
force which is to bring the most discord-
ant thinkers into sympathy with one
another. I mean the power of practical
work. We all know how the Church in
all its branches has wakened from its
lethargy and become aware of the misery
and sin of which the world is full, and
undertaken, with an energy which was
not known a few years ago, to do its duty.
It is an inspiring sight; and one of the
things which is most beautiful about it is
no doubt the way in which it unites in
practical benevolence men who are very
far apart in their ways of thinking and
believing. The Quaker and the Roman-
ist may stoop together to lift the drunk-
ard from the gutter. The Churchman
and the Agnostic may struggle side by
side against the pestilence of the grog-
shop and the filth of the tenement-house.
Nay, more; men who are utterly at vari-
ance about great points of theology may
plead with the same sinful and stricken

soul that it shall know the first great truths of the love of Christ and the waiting power of the Holy Spirit. All this is very good and noble. We rejoice in it with all our hearts. And just because we do rejoice in it, we want to be very clear about just what it is worth, and just what its limitations and its dangers are; for one of the greatest dangers to the purity and efficiency of any force is that it should be thought worth more than it is, and expected to do work for which it was not made. By and by men are sure to be found at the other extreme, thinking of the exaggerated force far less than it deserves.

The defect of Christian work as a means of Christian tolerance lies in its tendency to superficialness. I shall not be thought hostile or indifferent to the great bustle and glow of activity which fills our Church's life to-day if I remind you, who in a year or two will be in the very thick of it, that it must be backed and sup-

ported by thought and study and ideas,
or it becomes very thin indeed. One
must sometimes fear lest machineries
should take the place of truths, and lest
the necessity for instant action should
crowd out the possibility of earnest
thought in a Church so pressed upon by
need and so aware of duty as, God be
thanked! our Church is to-day. But men
must think; and the meeting of men with
men, of souls with souls, must ultimately
be upon the broad and open ground of
thought. And unless I can do more than
simply forget for a time my differences
from my brother thinker, while we both
stop our thinking in order to set some
moral evil right; unless I can, clearly
facing the fact of our difference, welcome
it, honor the spirit of his thought, seek
for enlightenment on my own thought
from his, and not dream of even wishing
to silence or to change his thought
except by reason, — unless I gain by
my fellow-work with him that precious

harmony between personal conviction and cordial sympathy, I am not growing tolerant. Tolerance does not mean the forgetting of differences, but the clear recognition of them and the hearty acceptance and use of them.

It is possible for the fellowship of work to help us to all that; and when it does so, it is good indeed. It must not sacrifice personal conviction to immediate efficiency. It must take those who join in doing it deep down into that underworld where personal convictions find the everlasting principles of which they are the individual expressions. It must invade and not evade the world of thought. It must reach and live in the unity which lies below, and not the unity which lies above, the puzzling questions of the soul. So only is its work thorough and permanent. So only does work bring tolerance. So only do the mission and the hospital and the parish machinery, the men's clubs and the mother's meetings, become good for the soul. Such power may work have with you, my friends, forever enlarging and opening your deepest lives.

Thus I have tried in these two lectures to speak of the nature, the methods, and the prospects of tolerance. If I have at all succeeded in what I have undertaken to do, one conviction, of which I just spoke as I closed the other evening, must have grown stronger and stronger in you as I have spoken. That conviction is that tolerance is not a special quality or attainment of life so much as it is an utterance of the life itself. Intolerance is meagreness of life. He whose life grows abundant, grows into sympathy with the lives of fellow-men, as when one pool among the many on the sea-shore rocks fills itself full, it overflows and becomes one with the other pools, making them also one with each other all over the broad expanse.

What then we need is fuller life. There is no word of Christ more tempting to any man who craves the largest and healthiest relations with his fellow-men than that word which is written in the tenth chapter of St. John: "I am come that they might have life, and that they might have it more abundantly." We may adjust relations as we will; we may decide just how far we can co-operate with this or that heretic; we may draw careful distinctions between the various classes of opinions about which we differ, labelling some essential, and some non-essential. It is all surface-work; it is all uncertain; it is full of mischief and of blunders; it is always joining together souls which have no sympathy with one another, and throwing apart souls which ought to be parts of each other's life. Only a deeper vitality, a richer filling of our spirits with the Spirit of God; an assurance of the possible divineness of the human life by an experience of how

richly it may be filled with divinity, —
only this can make us be to our brethren and make them be to us all that
God designed.

My friends, be more afraid of the littleness than of the largeness of life. Let
that be your rule about your people when
you come to be their minister.

Never let yourself think, and never al-
low them to think, that mere intolerance
upon their part, mere bitterness against
those who differ from them or from their
Church, is faith.

Never discourage them from thinking.
If they are thinking wrong, do not try to
stop their thinking, but teach them to
think right.

Never doubt their capacity for the best
faith, the profoundest experience, the largest liberty.

And for yourself, let the same rule be
master. Be more afraid of the littleness
than of the largeness of life. Seek with
study and with prayer for the most clear

and confident convictions; and when you have won them, hold them so largely and vitally that they shall be to you, not the walls which separate you from your brethren who have other convictions than yours, but the medium through which you enter into understanding of and sympathy with them, as the ocean, which once was the barrier between the nations, is now the highway for their never-resting ships, and makes the whole world one.

This is true tolerance. Into a deeper and deeper abundance of that tolerance may our Master lead all of us whom He has called to be His ministers!